LIBERTY

LYNN CURLEE

ALADDIN PAPERBACKS
New York   London   Toronto   Sydney   Singapore

LIBERTY

The New Colossus

Not like the brazen giant of Greek fame,
With conquering limbs astride from land to land;
Here at our sea-washed, sunset gates shall stand
A mighty woman with a torch, whose flame
Is the imprisoned lightning, and her name
Mother of Exiles. From her beacon-hand
Glows world-wide welcome; her mild eyes command
The air-bridged harbor that twin cities frame.
"Keep, ancient lands, your storied pomp!" cries she
With silent lips. "Give me your tired, your poor,
Your huddled masses yearning to breathe free,
The wretched refuse of your teeming shore.
Send these, the homeless, tempest-tost, to me,
I lift my lamp beside the golden door!"

—Emma Lazarus, 1883

She stands high above the water on her stone pedestal atop an abandoned fortress on a small island in Upper New York Bay. From here, where the mighty Hudson River empties into the sea, nearly two miles from the southern tip of Manhattan, she commands the bustling port, one of the world's greatest natural harbors. Draped in the heavy robes of an ancient Roman goddess, she seems to move forward, her sandals treading upon broken chains, which symbolize the forces of oppression and tyranny. In her left arm she cradles the tablet of law, inscribed "July 4, 1776," in Roman numerals. In her right hand she holds high a torch, which shines with the golden flame of freedom. On her head she wears a crown bristling with seven spiky rays, representing the seven continents and the seven seas. She is not pretty, but she is beautiful, her features majestic and severe, her glance stern and full of concentration.

The great lady was constructed more than 100 years ago. Made of iron and copper, she once gleamed reddish-brown, like a new penny, but decades of sun, wind, rain, and ice have turned her surface a flat, streaky pale green—the rich patina that copper acquires over time. She is the most colossal metal statue ever made, and over the course of a century she has become perhaps the most famous and beloved sculpture in the world.

She began as the symbol of an idea. Her creators gave her the title *Liberty Enlightening the World*. But later a young poet gave her another name, one less grand but more human and personal: Mother of Exiles. Facing east toward the Old World, she welcomes all who enter New York Harbor, gateway to the New World. For generations they have come seeking a better way of life, seeking freedom. She represents that freedom. For people all over the world, the Statue of Liberty is the symbol of America.

Surprisingly, America's symbol is French. The idea of a French professor, the Statue of Liberty was designed by a French sculptor and a French engineer, fabricated by French craftsmen, and paid for by the contributions of French citizens. She was a gift from the people of France to the people of the United States—a monument to the first 100 years of American independence and a gesture of friendship between two nations.

In the late 1700s, both countries experienced revolution, but the American Revolution led to the establishment of a stable republican form of government, in which representatives elected by the citizens make the decisions. The French Revolution, though originally based upon ideals of liberty, equality, and brotherhood, had led instead to a bloody Reign of Terror, the disastrous wars of Napoleon, and decades of bad government. Many patriotic Frenchmen longed for a republic patterned on that of America to replace their current regime, the Second Empire of Napoleon III. One of the most prominent patriots was Édouard de Laboulaye, a famous law professor and expert on American history.

It was in 1865, during a dinner party at his home near Versailles, that Laboulaye first proposed that a monument "be built in America as a memorial to their independence . . . by a united effort . . . the common work of both nations." One of the dinner guests that evening was a thirty-one-year-old sculptor named Frédéric-Auguste Bartholdi. The young man was

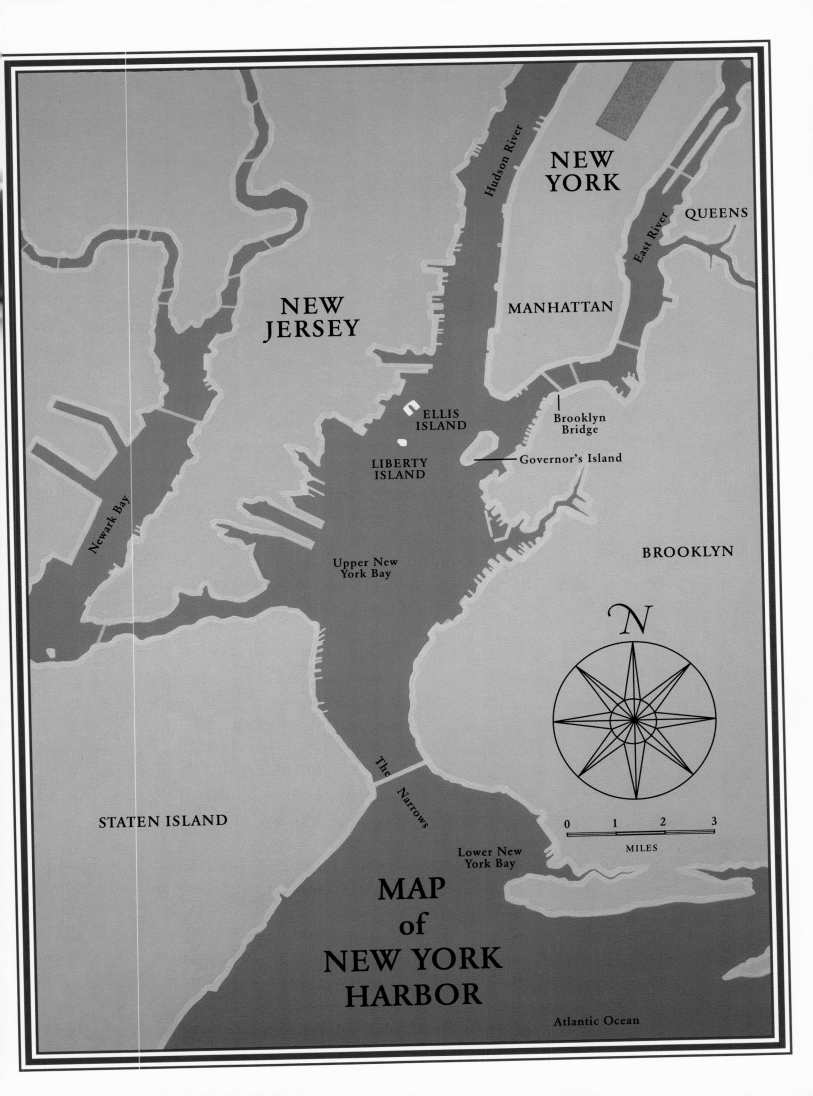

gripped at once by Laboulaye's idea. He said later that it became "fixed" in his mind. It was to become his obsession.

Auguste Bartholdi was a charming and dapper man. Slender, dark-haired, and elegant, he was enthusiastic, energetic, talented and passionately patriotic. He was born in 1834 in Alsace, a region of France which has, at various times, been under German rule. His family were well-to-do landowners. When Auguste was a boy, his father died and his strong-willed mother, Charlotte, became the family matriarch. She recognized her son's artistic talent and sent him to Paris to study.

Young Bartholdi was attracted to a heroic, monumental kind of art, in which lofty ideals are symbolized by figures inspired by the sculpture of ancient Greece and Rome. Called neoclassicism, this style of art was considered especially suitable for large public monuments and memorials. In 1856, the young artist made a journey to Egypt, where he was dazzled by the huge scale of ancient monuments such as the Pyramids and the Sphinx, and it became his ambition to sculpt great public works. When Auguste opened his own studio, his talent was recognized immediately, and he began receiving commissions. By 1865, the date of Laboulaye's dinner party, Bartholdi's reputation as a sculptor was well established, but the time was not right for a French tribute to liberty. The Second Empire frowned upon democratic ideas. But the seed had been planted; for the next ten years it would grow in Bartholdi's imagination.

Meanwhile his career thrived. It was during a second trip to Egypt in 1869 that Bartholdi made a startling proposal to the Egyptian govern-

ment: He would erect a lighthouse at the entrance to the Suez Canal, then under construction. It would have the form of a colossal Egyptian peasant woman and bear the title *Egypt Bringing the Light to Asia*. Nothing came of this proposal, but it shows that in his mind Bartholdi was already working out the design that would eventually become the Statue of Liberty.

In August 1870, France was invaded by Germany. The Franco-Prussian War forced Bartholdi home to Alsace, where German soldiers had occupied his mother's home. Appointed head of the local French troops, Bartholdi endured the humiliation of personally surrendering his hometown of Colmar to the enemy. In 1871, with the end of the war and the fall of Napoleon III, conditions finally seemed ripe for a French Republic. Laboulaye was convinced that a Statue of Liberty would help rally the French people, and Bartholdi decided to attack his "American project" head-on. He left France armed with letters of introduction from Laboulaye to many prominent Americans.

His ship sailed into New York Harbor at dawn on June 21, 1871: "The sky grew pink—a multitude of little sails seemed to skim the water—our fellow travelers pointed out a cloud of smoke at the farther end of the bay—it was New York!" As his ship approached Manhattan, Bartholdi turned his attention to a small island guarded by the walls of an old fortress. Bedloe's Island, named for its original Dutch owner, was the property of the United States government. At his very first sight of America, Bartholdi had found what he wanted—the perfect place to build his vision of Liberty. He later said, "At the view of the harbor . . .

the definite plan was first clear to my eyes. Here . . . my statue must rise; here where people get their first view of the New World." It would take fifteen years more to turn his vision into reality.

For the next months, as he traveled from coast to coast, Bartholdi visited most of America's major cities. Thanks to Laboulaye's connections, he met many prominent people, including President Ulysses S. Grant. He described his vision to everyone he met, and although he encountered some indifference and even skepticism, he also made many friends and found much support. He returned to France encouraged and more determined than ever.

Although he had had a basic idea for Liberty and started sketching and modeling before his American trip, the experience of New York Harbor and the sight of Bedloe's Island had focused Bartholdi's creative energy. Over the next three months, he made a series of large terra-cotta maquettes, or models, gradually refining his design. In the first maquettes, Liberty's figure is more graceful. There is no tablet of law, and the rays of her crown point up instead of out. In later models she is more severe, the tablet has been added, and the magnificent spikes of her crown stand straight out from her head like rays of light. According to tradition, Bartholdi used his own mother as the model for Liberty's face.

In planning Liberty, Bartholdi was always well aware of one important historical precedent: one of the traditional Seven Wonders of the World was also a gigantic statue that stood guard at the entrance to a harbor. The Colossus of Rhodes was erected in the third century B.C. It represented the figure of the Greek sun god, Helios. Made of cast bronze, it stood for just a half century before it was toppled by an earthquake. We know it only from written descriptions that tell us it was made in segments and stood 110 feet tall, including its base. We know that one arm was raised, but otherwise we do not know exactly how it looked. We do know that in Greek art, Helios was usually shown with a crown of rays. Bartholdi knew that his work would be compared with the famous ancient statue, and he was determined that his Liberty would be a colossus for the modern world. Early in 1875 he finished his final terra-cotta maquette. Nearly five feet tall, this was the model from which Liberty's proportions would be taken.

Now it was time to do business because statues cost money. In 1875, Laboulaye had set up the French-American Union, an organization to raise funds for the project. Bartholdi's final maquette was unveiled at a lavish banquet given by the Union on November 6, 1875, at the Hôtel du Louvre in Paris. The dinner raised 40,000 francs, and by the end of the year, the French-American Union had received contributions totaling 200,000 francs. Now it was official: Bartholdi could begin the greatest challenge of his life, building a hollow metal statue more than 150 feet tall.

Fabricating Liberty was a very complex process involving many different artisans and craftsmen—sculptors, plasterers, carpenters, and metalsmiths. Two weeks after the banquet, Bartholdi met with members of the craftsmen's guild, and arrangements were made to start work at once. They would begin with the right arm and torch of Liberty for display at

the Philadelphia Centennial Exposition, which was held the following summer.

Bartholdi had decided to make his immense statue out of copper. Copper is lighter and cheaper than bronze, it is very malleable, and it can be beautifully worked in thin sheets. These sheets of copper would be assembled like a gigantic puzzle to form Liberty's surface, and would be supported by some kind of armature, which had not yet been determined. In this way Liberty could be made in segments, although it seems astonishing today that Bartholdi actually started building Liberty without knowing exactly what would hold her up. The copper was worked in an ancient technique called repoussé ("pushed back" in French), in which the thin metal sheet was hammered into a form or mold to make the correct shape. In order to make the forms, a full-scale model of Liberty had to be prepared.

The first step was to enlarge the final terra-cotta maquette. This was done in stages by a process called pointing. A box-like wooden framework was built around the top and bottom of the original model, which was marked with a grid of points. The height, width, and depth of each point was measured from the framework. Another framework was constructed, similar to the first, but at a larger scale. The measurements of each point were multiplied to fit the new scale, and an enlarged copy was gradually built up within the second framework from plaster applied over a wooden support. To enlarge Liberty, this tedious and exacting process was repeated three times, requiring the precise measurement of thousands of points. The first enlargement was double the size of the original maquette—more than nine feet tall. This model was then enlarged to be exactly four times bigger,

thirty-eight feet tall. Due to the immense scale, for the final enlargement the thirty-eight foot model was divided into segments, each of which was then enlarged to be four times bigger than the last. When assembled, the finished statue would be more than 151 feet tall. But in 1876 only the arm and torch were enlarged to full scale.

When the pointers, sculptors, and plasterers finished the segments of the full-scale model, the carpenters and wood-carvers constructed the wooden forms for the repoussé work directly against the plaster surface of the model. These forms resembled surrealistic bookcases, with slats of wood sawed and carved to follow every curve and bend of the plaster model, matching it exactly but in reverse. The forms were then removed and coppersmiths took over, using levers, mallets, and hammers to force the sheets of metal, each about the thickness of a silver dollar, into every nook and cranny of the forms, reproducing the shape of the plaster model, but this time in copper. The plates of metal made from the different forms were riveted together to make Liberty's "skin." The finished statue would be made up of more than 350 segments, held together by more than 600,000 rivets.

Twenty craftsmen labored ten hours a day, seven days a week for months to prepare the arm and torch in time for the Philadelphia Exposition's opening in May 1876. But it was not until June that the thirty-foot section stood complete, the shiny copper glinting under Bartholdi's studio skylight. It was shipped to Philadelphia in August and became one of the Exposition's great attractions. Bartholdi came as well and spent eight

months in the United States, raising funds and finding support for Liberty. On February 22, 1877, Congress voted to accept *Liberty Enlightening the World* as a gift from France, and to provide the site as well as funds for maintenance. In addition, a proper pedestal was needed for the gigantic statue, so the American Committee for the Statue of Liberty was formed to raise the money and engage an architect.

When the Philadelphia Exposition was over, the torch was moved to New York's Madison Square Park, where it was open to visitors for a fee of fifty cents. It remained on display in New York until the rest of Liberty was nearly finished.

Bartholdi's second American visit had been a great success, and he even married during the trip. Jeanne-Emilie Baheux de Puysieux was a lovely young Frenchwoman who Bartholdi had met during his first American visit. After she and Auguste had fallen in love and married, it was rumored that she had served as the model for Liberty's shapely arms and beautiful, expressive hands.

Bartholdi returned with his bride to France in early 1877. He immediately engaged the firm of Gaget, Gauthier and Company, master metalsmiths, to continue with Liberty's fabrication. The head was the next section to be enlarged and duplicated in copper. Bartholdi planned to exhibit it at the Paris Universal Exposition of 1878. After more than a year of intense labor in the workshops of Gaget, the head was finished, and in June, 1878, it was moved through the streets of Paris to the Champ de Mars, site of the exposition. Drawn on a huge cart by thirteen massive draft horses, the enormous head was cushioned by a thick bed of hay and

twigs, which allowed it to rock slightly. At every bump and turn Liberty seemed to nod to the cheering throngs.

She created a sensation at the exposition, where, for a fee, visitors could climb to the top and look out the windows of Liberty's crown. Money to continue the statue was raised in other ways, too. Replicas of the statue, signed by Bartholdi, were sold, as were the rights to use her image. Finally, the French-American Union held a lottery with prizes donated by prosperous French businesses. On July 7, 1880, Laboulaye announced that enough money had been raised to complete the statue, which cost a total of about $600,000 in 1880s dollars.

Until now Bartholdi had proceeded without a plan for the most critical part of Liberty's construction. She is so immense that her thin copper shell weighs more than thirty-two tons. Without some kind of internal support, she would simply collapse. Early in 1880, Bartholdi approached French engineer Alexandre-Gustave Eiffel and asked him to tackle the problem.

Eiffel, two years older than Bartholdi, was one of the great geniuses in the history of engineering. He had pioneered the use of iron for large-scale construction in a series of bridges for the French railway system. Eiffel built the elegant spans and the supporting towers or pylons of his bridges out of iron girders arranged in latticelike grids. In the mid-nineteenth century this was a new and truly revolutionary idea. Structures built in this way could support a great weight, and they could be very tall. Known as the "Magician of Iron," Eiffel immediately set to work designing Liberty's

LIBERTY ENLIGHTENING THE WORLD

DESIGN FOR THE INTERNAL IRON FRAMEWORK

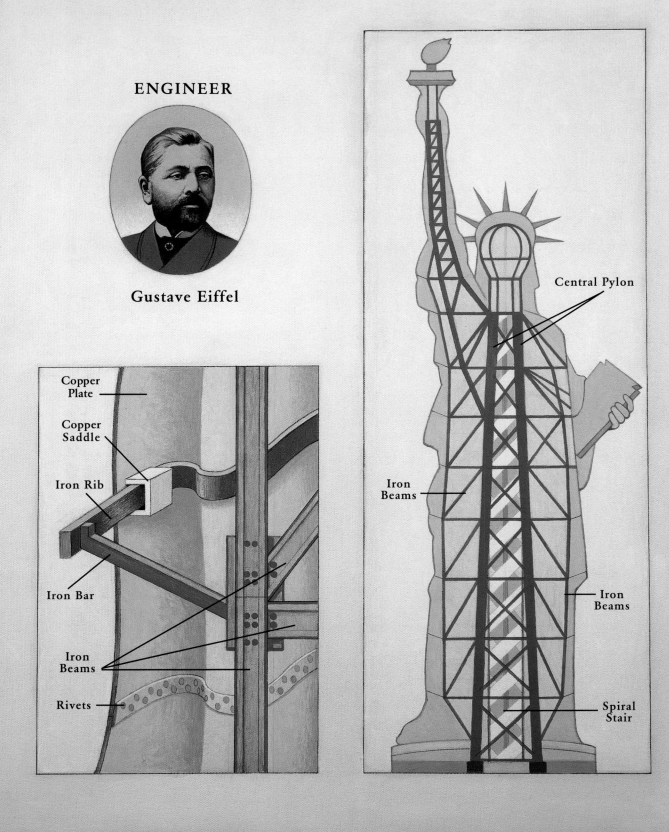

ENGINEER

Gustave Eiffel

Copper Plate

Copper Saddle

Iron Rib

Iron Bar

Iron Beams

Rivets

Central Pylon

Iron Beams

Iron Beams

Spiral Stair

armature, using the principles he had developed for his bridges.

In the center he placed a tall pylon made of four large vertical iron beams connected by cross braces. A skeleton of thinner iron beams was bolted to the outside of the pylon. From this framework, short iron bars sprang out to the copper plates of Liberty's skin. Each plate was backed by iron ribs, each forged to match the inside shape of the copper, and these ribs were bolted to the short iron bars. In this way each copper plate was "hung" from the iron framework, and its weight was transferred to the central pylon, not to the plates below. The iron ribs were not connected directly to the plates, but rather passed through copper "saddles," which *were* attached, allowing the rigid metal to flex and move in high winds or with changes in temperature. In the very center, Eiffel constructed a double-spiral staircase, with one stair for ascending and the other for descending. With Liberty's armature Eiffel had invented a completely new and ingenious method of construction called the "curtain wall." Within a few years this system was used by architects to build the first skyscrapers. (In 1889, Eiffel would build his masterpiece, a spectacular tower of iron nearly one thousand feet high, for another Paris exposition. The Eiffel Tower was the tallest structure in the world until 1930, when it was topped by New York's Chrysler Building.)

During 1881, while iron workers constructed the enormous framework of Liberty's armature in the courtyard of Gaget, Gauthier and Company, the craftsmen inside continued to fabricate the statue. As many as fifty people could be working on various parts of the statue at the same time. With the torch arm and the head already complete, the body of the

thirty-eight-foot model was divided into eight segments, like the layers of a cake. Each segment was enlarged separately and duplicated in copper, starting at the feet and moving up. As each segment was finished, its copper plates were hoisted into place and attached to the armature. Gradually, over the next two years, the gigantic figure took shape. In the autumn of 1883, the head was installed, and the right arm and torch, which had been shipped back to Paris from New York, were lifted into place and attached during the winter. By February 1884, Bartholdi was able to write to the American Committee that "our statue is completed." For the next year, the gleaming copper colossus of *Liberty Enlightening the World* loomed over the rooftops of Paris.

But in the United States things were not proceeding quite so smoothly. Charged in 1877 with providing a suitable pedestal for Liberty, the American Committee had moved very slowly. They did not choose an architect or even begin raising funds until 1882, while Liberty was being erected in France. Then early that year, the committee asked Richard Morris Hunt to design the pedestal. As a young man Hunt was the first American ever to study architecture at the École des Beaux-Arts in Paris. He made his reputation building opulent mansions for New York's most fashionable and wealthy people. Like Bartholdi, Hunt worked in the "Grand Manner," taking design elements from different periods of history and combining them.

Liberty needed a tall, massive base to complement her huge scale and to anchor her firmly to the ground. Hunt's first design was nearly 115 feet

tall, and it was estimated that such a pedestal would cost approximately $250,000. But the American Committee was having trouble raising money. By the end of 1883, only one-third of this amount was available, and Hunt changed his design several times before a final plan was approved with a more economical height of eighty-nine feet. Hunt's design called for a tapered concrete mass, faced in granite blocks, with classical decorations. In the meantime, excavations were begun for the pedestal's foundation in the center of old Fort Wood, the obsolete military post on Bedloe's Island. While digging an enormous pit twenty feet deep for the foundation, the engineers encountered rubble and underground rooms. All of this had to be removed, which cost more time and money, and the members of the American Committee began to quarrel among themselves.

On July 4, 1884, the completed statue was formally presented to the American people in a ceremony held at her feet in the courtyard of Gaget, Gauthier and Company. According to the Paris Morning News, after some eloquent speeches "the illustrious company, with Monsieur Bartholdi leading the way, visited the statue by entering by the door in the sole of the upraised foot, and toiling readily up the double staircase with nothing to guide their steps but the ten thousand little eyelets of sunlight that came through the rivet holes." The article went on to describe the dignitaries as "pygmies wandering about the interior of the monster." One very important person was absent, however: Edouard de Laboulaye had died in 1883.

Workmen began dismantling the statue for transport to America in January 1885. Every piece of metal was marked to show its position in the

statue, and Liberty's parts were packed into 214 crates. It took a train with seventy cars to transport her to the harbor at Rouen. The crates were loaded onto the *Isère*, a French naval ship. After nearly a month at sea, the *Isère* entered New York Harbor on June 19, where she was met by a flotilla of ships and small boats. One newspaper wrote, "The guns from Bedloe's Island crashed with a deafening noise . . . a hundred steam-whistles shrieked, and 10,000 people waved handkerchiefs and flags." There was real cause for the jubilation—only three months before, the entire Liberty project had been in jeopardy.

One month after the July 4th ceremony in Paris the year before, the cornerstone for the pedestal had been laid in the completed foundation on Bedloe's Island, and construction had begun. But soon the American Committee had run out of money and construction was halted on the pedestal. An additional $100,000 was needed to complete Liberty's base. Bartholdi was dismayed. Would his completed work find a home in New York Harbor after all?

But at this point, in a dramatic turn of events, Liberty's cause was taken up by Joseph Pulitzer, owner of *The World*, one of New York's daily newspapers. In his youth Pulitzer had immigrated to America from Hungary. By 1883, he owned several newspapers. Beginning on March 15, 1885, Pulitzer ran a series of editorials blasting the wealthy, who had given little to the pedestal fund, and appealed directly to the common man to contribute: "Let us not wait for the millionaires. . . . Give something, however little. . . . We will publish the name of every giver, however small the sum given."

And the money began flowing in. By May, when the *Isère* sailed from France, enough had been raised to resume work. Then on August 11, *The World* ran a bold headline:

ONE HUNDRED THOUSAND DOLLARS

TRIUMPHANT COMPLETION OF THE

WORLD'S FUND FOR THE LIBERTY PEDESTAL

In five months, 121,000 people had contributed $102,000. Working men and women, the elderly, the poor, immigrants, and children sent their dollars and their pennies. Pulitzer published every name. Now Liberty truly belonged to the American people.

It would be one more year before Liberty stood complete in New York Harbor. The pedestal was finished by April 1886. During the next two months, the iron armature was reassembled atop the pedestal and bolted to huge girders embedded in the concrete of the base. Then on July 12, the workmen began attaching the copper plates. Some of the copper had sagged out of shape while in storage and had to be reworked. Workmen, seated in sling chairs suspended high above the wind-swept harbor, struggled to reassemble the great statue. Even so, work proceeded without major problems, and finally, on October 25, 1886, the last rivet was driven into place. The Statue of Liberty was finished at last, twenty-one years after Laboulaye's dinner party.

Dedication Day, October 28, 1886, dawned gray and drizzly. The great statue was shrouded in mist, her face veiled by an enormous French tri-

color flag. The city streets were thronged with people, and the harbor teemed with ships and pleasure boats filled with spectators. After a festive parade down Fifth Avenue, a naval procession ferried the official party to Bedloe's Island for the dedication ceremony. Among the dignitaries on board were Bartholdi and his wife, who had arrived in New York three days before, and the president of the United States, Grover Cleveland. When introduced to Bartholdi, the president said, "You are the greatest man in America today."

One boat was full of protestors. Today it seems incredible, but no women were invited to the unveiling except for the wives of the French officials. A group of suffragists campaigning for women's rights positioned their boat directly in front of the viewing stand to point out the supreme irony that a statue dedicated to the idea of liberty was in the form of a woman at a time when women were denied even the basic right to vote— a right women would finally win in 1920.

The honor of unveiling Liberty's face would go to the artist himself. According to the newspapers: "Every eye now watched the flag that enveloped the colossal face of the statue that towered so grandly above. The clouds of mist and smoke and steam rolled around and enveloped it like the smoke of battles in which liberty was born." In the middle of one of the numerous speeches, signals were mixed, and Bartholdi pulled the cord at the wrong moment: "Suddenly the tricolor vanished and looking down through the fog and rain was that mighty human face. At that moment from the guns of the men-of-war burst forth a tremendous salvo of artillery and all the steam whistles in the flotilla blew as they never

blew before." It was like "a hundred Fourths of July." Three nights later, floodlights illuminated the burnished copper figure of Liberty, which was the centerpiece of a brilliant display of fireworks. When the great celebration was over, Auguste Bartholdi simply said, "The dream of my life is accomplished."

As the symbol of an idea, *Liberty Enlightening the World* is grand and inspiring. The Frenchmen who made her were expressing the conviction that personal freedom is best achieved through a democratic form of government. But it was a young woman who provided the immense construction of hard, cold metal with a heart and soul and voice.

In 1883, as part of their fund-raising effort, the American Committee had held a literary auction in New York. Some manuscripts by noted writers were included. One of the contributors was a young poet named Emma Lazarus, daughter of a wealthy New York businessman. Inspired by the plight of Russian immigrants who had fled to America to escape terrible persecution, she composed a sonnet entitled "The New Colossus." In rich, poetic language she contrasts the ancient Colossus of Rhodes ("the brazen giant . . . with conquering limbs") with the Statue of Liberty, which she calls "Mother of Exiles." The poem's "air-bridged harbor" refers to the newly completed Brooklyn Bridge, the engineering marvel of the age, which joined the "Twin Cities" of New York and Brooklyn. In the coming decades Emma Lazarus's poem would be understood to express the ultimate meaning of the statue—that America, the home of the free, is the haven of the oppressed.

In the late nineteenth and early twentieth centuries, wave after wave of European immigrants entered the United States. Millions of men, women, and children came in thousands of ships, and all of them passed directly beneath the Statue of Liberty as they sailed into New York Harbor. In 1892, six years after Liberty's dedication, nearby Ellis Island became the official entry station for all of these people. And they all took the great statue into their hearts as the symbol of a new life in a new land full of opportunity and promise. It is estimated that nearly 40 percent of all Americans living today can trace their ancestry to people who landed at Ellis Island in the shadow of the Statue of Liberty, Mother of Exiles. In 1903, the words of "The New Colossus" were engraved on a plaque that was installed in Liberty's pedestal, forever linking the statue and the poem.

As for the statue itself, over the years, as it gradually weathered to a lovely pale green, there have been a few minor changes and additions. The most extensive work was done on the torch. Bartholdi had sculpted the flame as a solid form, with the intention of having it gilded. Instead, Liberty's American engineers cut small portholes in the flame and installed lights, but the lights were too dim and the effect was very poor. In 1916, the flame was completely reworked by Gutzon Borglum, the sculptor who would later design the Mount Rushmore memorial. He cut away large panels of copper and filled the holes with panes of glass, turning the flame into a kind of giant Tiffany lamp. Over the years, as technology improved, the lighting system was upgraded several times.

In 1924, the statue was proclaimed a national monument, and in 1956, Bedloe's Island was renamed Liberty Island, as Bartholdi had always wished. Nine years later, Ellis Island, which had been closed in 1954, was made part of the Statue of Liberty National Monument.

After the celebration of the bicentennial of the United States in 1976, it became clear that the statue was in serious need of extensive and expensive repairs. In 1982, a fund-raising drive was begun to finance a complete restoration of America's symbol, and Liberty disappeared behind a cage of steel scaffolding that covered the statue and its pedestal completely.

The most serious problem was rust and corrosion. The statue had always leaked, and many of the forged iron ribs that support the copper panels had almost completely disintegrated. Every single rib was removed in turn and reproduced by hand in stainless steel, an enormous and exacting job. The entire torch arm had always been slightly out of line, even when the statue was first assembled in Paris, and the structural framework of the right shoulder was rebuilt to strengthen it. The interior of the statue had been painted at least seven times, and all the paint was stripped off by freezing it with liquid nitrogen. The copper was generally in excellent condition, and the exterior was cleaned and treated to prevent future corrosion. Each individual rivet was examined, and the loose or missing ones were replaced.

Besides the attention paid to the statue itself, the visitor facilities and museum exhibits were modernized and greatly improved. The double-spiral staircase was reworked, and a new heating and ventilation system was installed.

As a wonderful finishing touch, the torch itself was removed and replaced. French coppersmiths fabricated a new flame in the repoussé technique, copying Bartholdi's original design, and the flame was gilded with brilliant gold leaf, which seems to blaze even at night, illuminated by hidden floodlights. Finally, after three and a half years and $31 million, the scaffold was removed, and Liberty emerged in better condition and more beautiful than ever. At the age of 100, she was honored in 1986 with a gala ceremony and fireworks extravaganza as part of the July Fourth celebration, which was broadcast on television and reached an audience of millions of Americans. The statue was officially rededicated by President Ronald Reagan on October 28.

And so America's symbol stands today, still holding high her torch. Visitors from all over the world take the ferry to Liberty Island to climb the spiral stairs and gaze from the windows of Liberty's crown, and to wonder at the magnificent colossus of our modern age. Experts tell us that, with proper maintenance and by replacing individual pieces of metal as they wear out, the Statue of Liberty should stand for centuries. But, like freedom itself, she cannot be taken for granted; the great lady must be loved and cared for. As long as she lives in our hearts and minds, Liberty will enlighten the world.

SPECIFICATIONS

Height of the statue: 151 feet 1 inch
Height of the pedestal: 89 feet
Height of the foundation: 65 feet
Total height: 305 feet 1 inch
Height of the torch: 21 feet
Length of the tablet: 23 feet 7 inches
Width of the tablet: 13 feet 7 inches
Thickness of the tablet: 2 feet
Width of an eye: 2 feet 6 inches
Length of the nose: 4 feet 6 inches
Width of the mouth: 3 feet
Length of the right arm: 42 feet
Length of the hand: 16 feet 5 inches
Length of the forefinger: 8 feet
Size of the fingernail: 13 x 10 inches
Thickness of the copper: 1/8 to 3/32 inches
Weight of the copper: 32 tons
Weight of the iron: 125 tons
Steps in the statue: 171
Steps in the pedestal: 192
Cost of the statue (1880s dollars): $600,000
Cost of the pedestal (1880s dollars): $270,000
Cost of the restoration (1980s dollars): $31,000,000

Weights and dollar amounts are estimates and sometimes vary from source to source.